The Gardens

The Gardens

Based on Surah Al-Kahf (verses 32-44)

TIBS™ Method
(**T**eaching **I**slam **B**ased on **S**tories Method)

by
Fariba Kazemi

Noor House Publication

Toronto, Canada
www.noorhousepublication.com
@noorhousepublication

First edition published in 2024

Author: Fariba Kazemi
Translator: Maria Kashef
Illustrator: Shadi Hashemi
Graphic Designer: Nazanin Hosseinmardi
Editor: Aaron Wannamaker

Legal Deposit in year 2024 with Library Archive of Canada

The Gardens

ISBN: 978-1-7387615-2-4 (Paperback edition)
ISBN: 978-1-7387615-3-1 (eBook edition)

Published in Canada

In memory of my beloved brother,

Roozbeh,

who was a great patient warrior,

with a great passion for writing.

Content

About the Author

Fariba Kazemi is a storywriter and storyteller with a bachelor's degree in health care, living in Toronto.

While trying to raise her children as practicing Muslims in North America, **Fariba** founded **Noor House** in 2008 in order to encourage critical thinking and investigation of Islamic concepts in young minds.

Noor House is a non–profit organization dedicated to teaching Islam to children and adolescents.

After a few years of using different resources for teaching core Islamic values, she decided to establish a more creative and attractive method of teaching Islam that would better impress new generations. She called it the **TIBS**™ (Teaching Islam Based on Stories) method.

Introduction

Dear Reader:

This book includes two sections. The first section is for kids and the second for adults.

The first section includes a short story which is entertaining by itself for kids.

However, to gain the maximum benefit of the TIBS™ method of learning Quranic concepts, kids should follow the Learning Steps in the second section under the supervision of parents or teachers.

For further information on the TIBS method, its purpose, and how to use it, please refer to the Reader's Guide section.

Although this book is written for children in the age group of nine and above, adults can also enjoy and benefit from reading it.

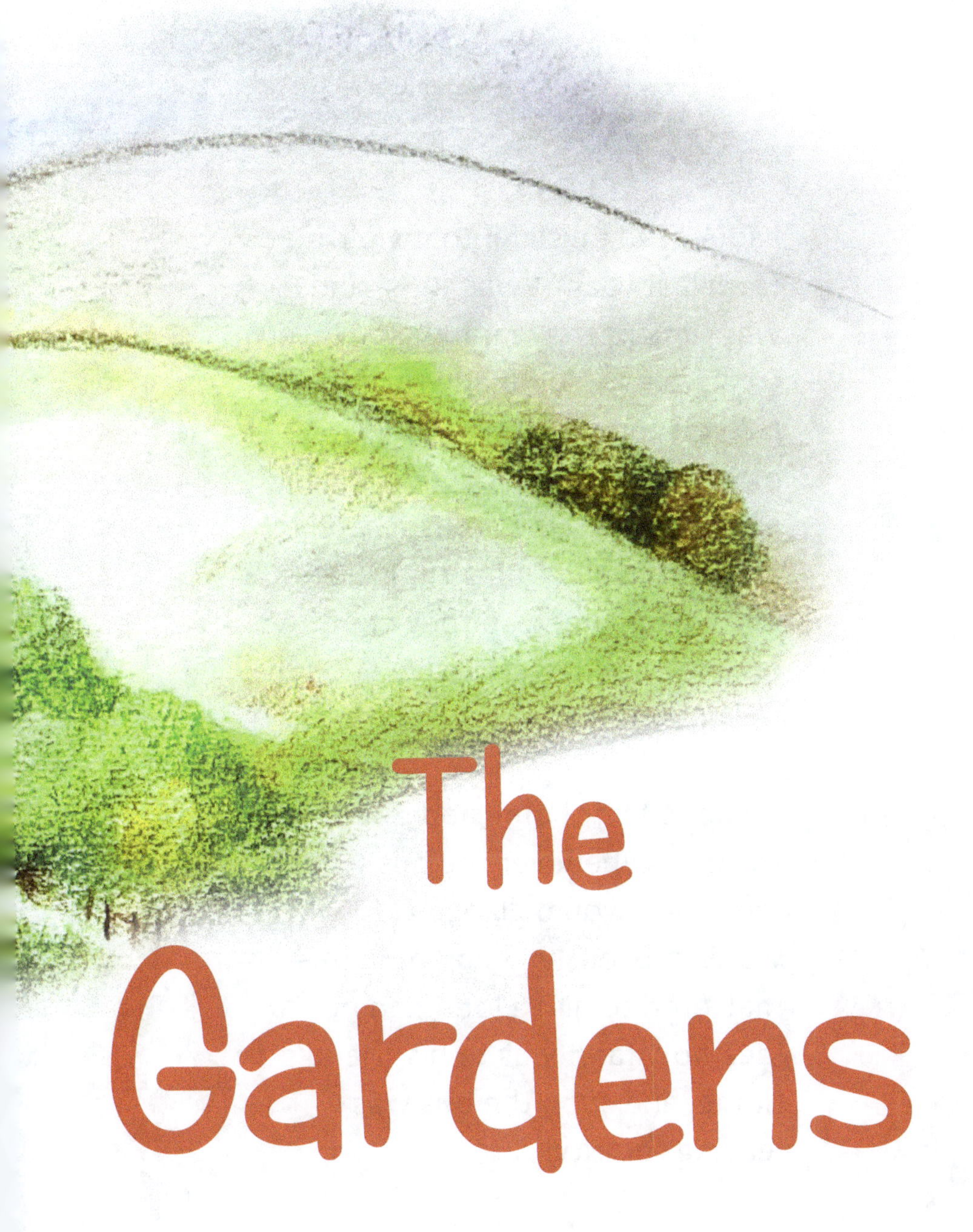

The Gardens

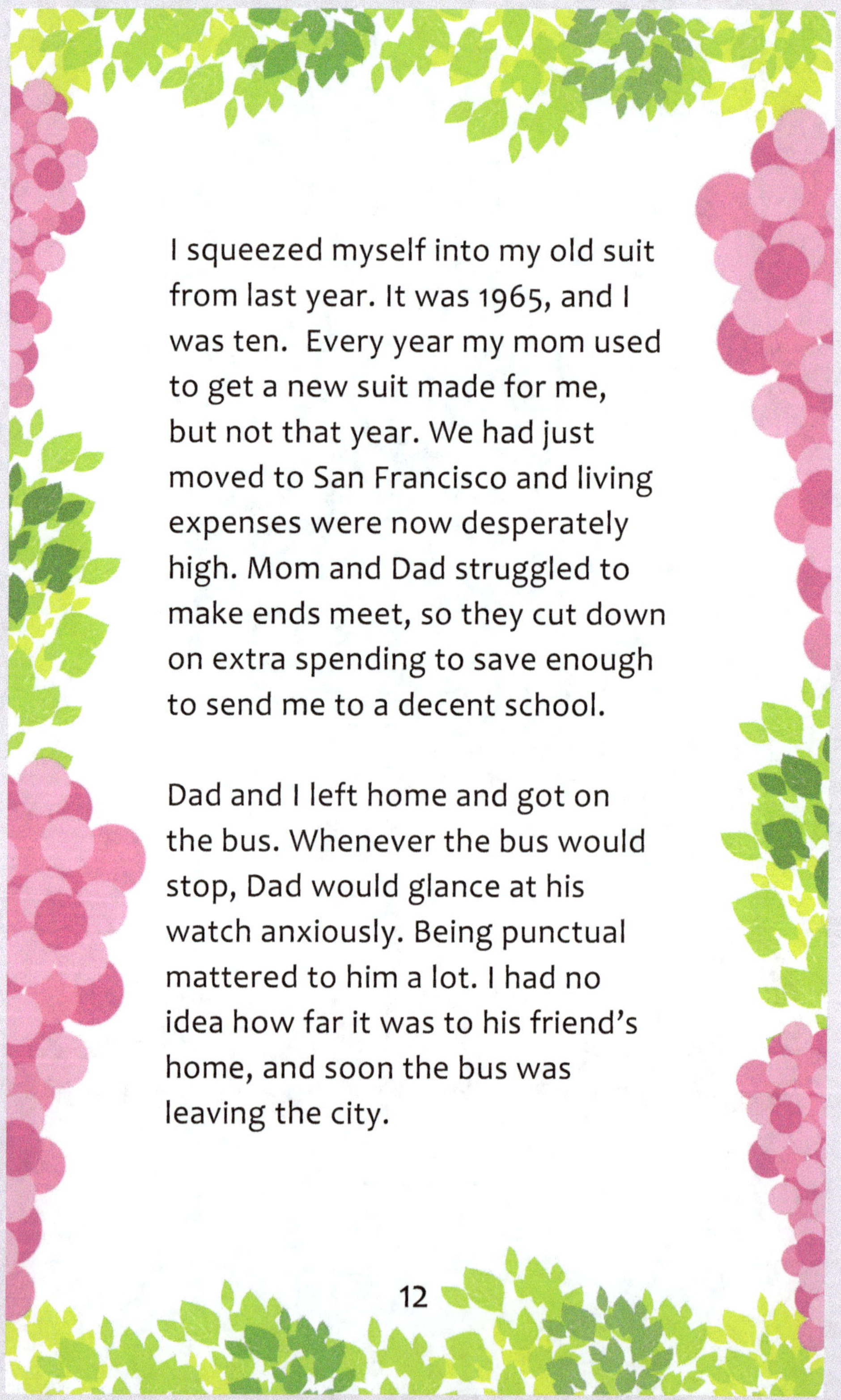

I squeezed myself into my old suit from last year. It was 1965, and I was ten. Every year my mom used to get a new suit made for me, but not that year. We had just moved to San Francisco and living expenses were now desperately high. Mom and Dad struggled to make ends meet, so they cut down on extra spending to save enough to send me to a decent school.

Dad and I left home and got on the bus. Whenever the bus would stop, Dad would glance at his watch anxiously. Being punctual mattered to him a lot. I had no idea how far it was to his friend's home, and soon the bus was leaving the city.

I felt drowsy and didn't even
realize I had fallen asleep until
Dad finally called me and we got
off the bus. There was no sign
of human habitation. Ahead of
us was a dirt path stretching far
to the lush green foothills of
the Napa Valley.

I looked at Dad and asked,
"Is this the right place?"

"I think so," he replied hesitantly, checking the directions he had written down on his notepad.

We started walking and that was enough to tarnish the beauty of my shiny shoes. Dad hailed a passing tractor and checked the directions with the driver. The driver offered to give us a ride and we sat in the back of the wagon that was

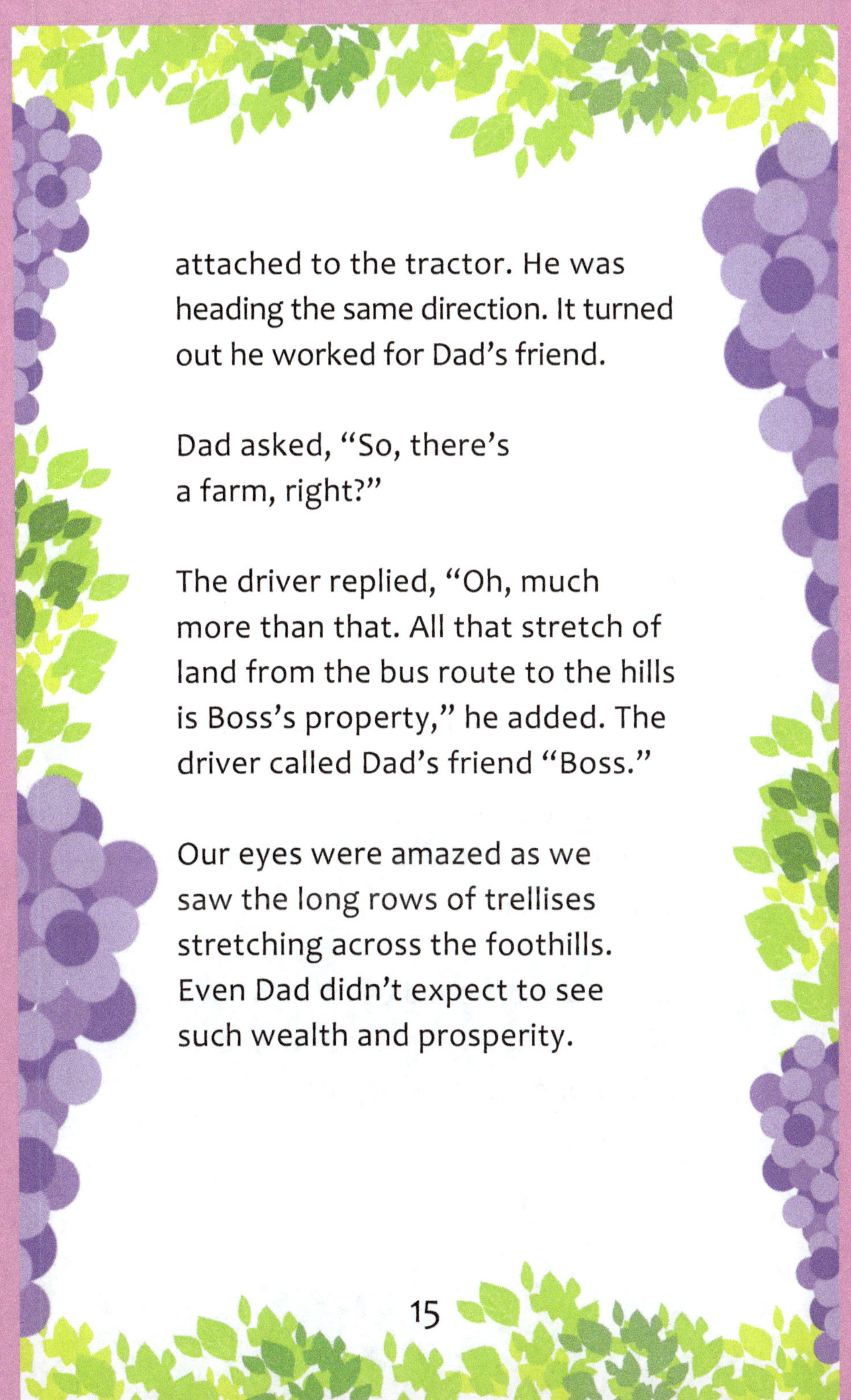

attached to the tractor. He was heading the same direction. It turned out he worked for Dad's friend.

Dad asked, "So, there's a farm, right?"

The driver replied, "Oh, much more than that. All that stretch of land from the bus route to the hills is Boss's property," he added. The driver called Dad's friend "Boss."

Our eyes were amazed as we saw the long rows of trellises stretching across the foothills. Even Dad didn't expect to see such wealth and prosperity.

Dad and Boss used to be close
friends in school but had gone their
own way to make their fortunes
20 years ago. Occasionally,
he and Boss exchanged cards
and kept in touch.

Over the years Dad worked his
way up to being an engineer,
and found work in San Francisco
helping to manage construction
of several new high-rise buildings.
Now that he and his friend
lived closer, they had a chance
to meet again.

The driver dropped us off in front
of a large gate. There was a small
telephone box by the gate,

and the driver picked up the
phone and spoke. The gate
opened a few seconds later.
A very green garden in its prime
was in front of us. At my age,
I felt like I was looking at Heaven.
The grapevines were neatly
arranged in rows with their
branches drooping over tall
trellises. Green and red grape

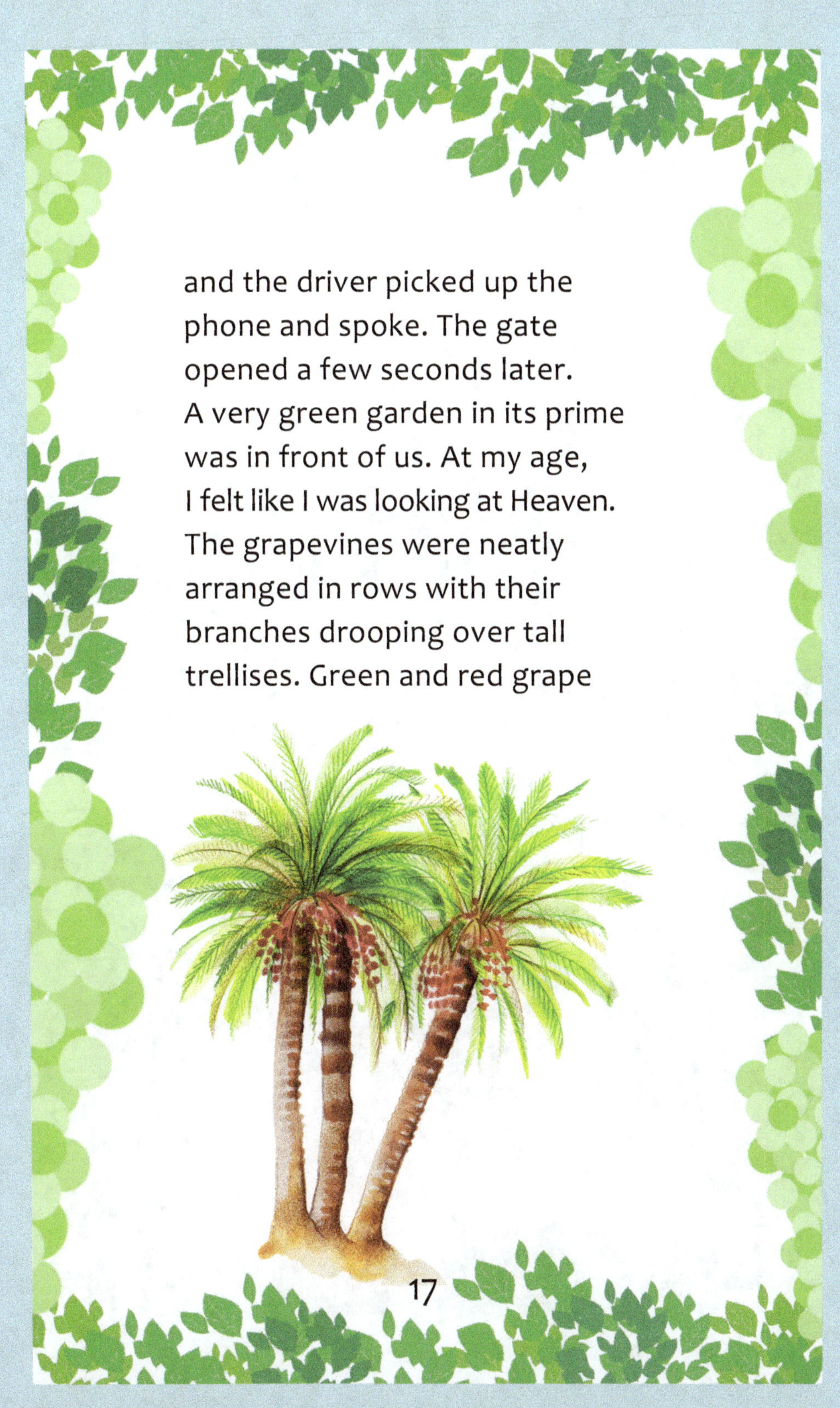

clusters were hanging loosely
from each trellis and were shining
in the sunshine like emeralds and
rubies. Around the perimeter were
lofty date palm trees surrounding
the garden like a wall. Bunches of
golden dates were hanging from
each tree. Everything showed a
good harvest and a fruitful year.

I said to Dad, "What a beautiful
garden! It looks like Paradise!"

Dad replied with a smile,
"It certainly is impressive.
As God wills."

At the far end of the cobblestone
road in front of us was a shining
white house.

A chubby man was standing
in front of it and waving at us.
When we got closer he opened
his arms, greeted us warmly,
and embraced Dad. I knew he
was Dad's friend, Boss.

"If I knew you didn't have a car,
I would have sent you one!"
Boss said. After that he gently
brushed his palm over my head
and asked, "Hey young man,
what's your name?"

"Zach," I replied.

Then he asked my dad, "Is this
your youngest child?"

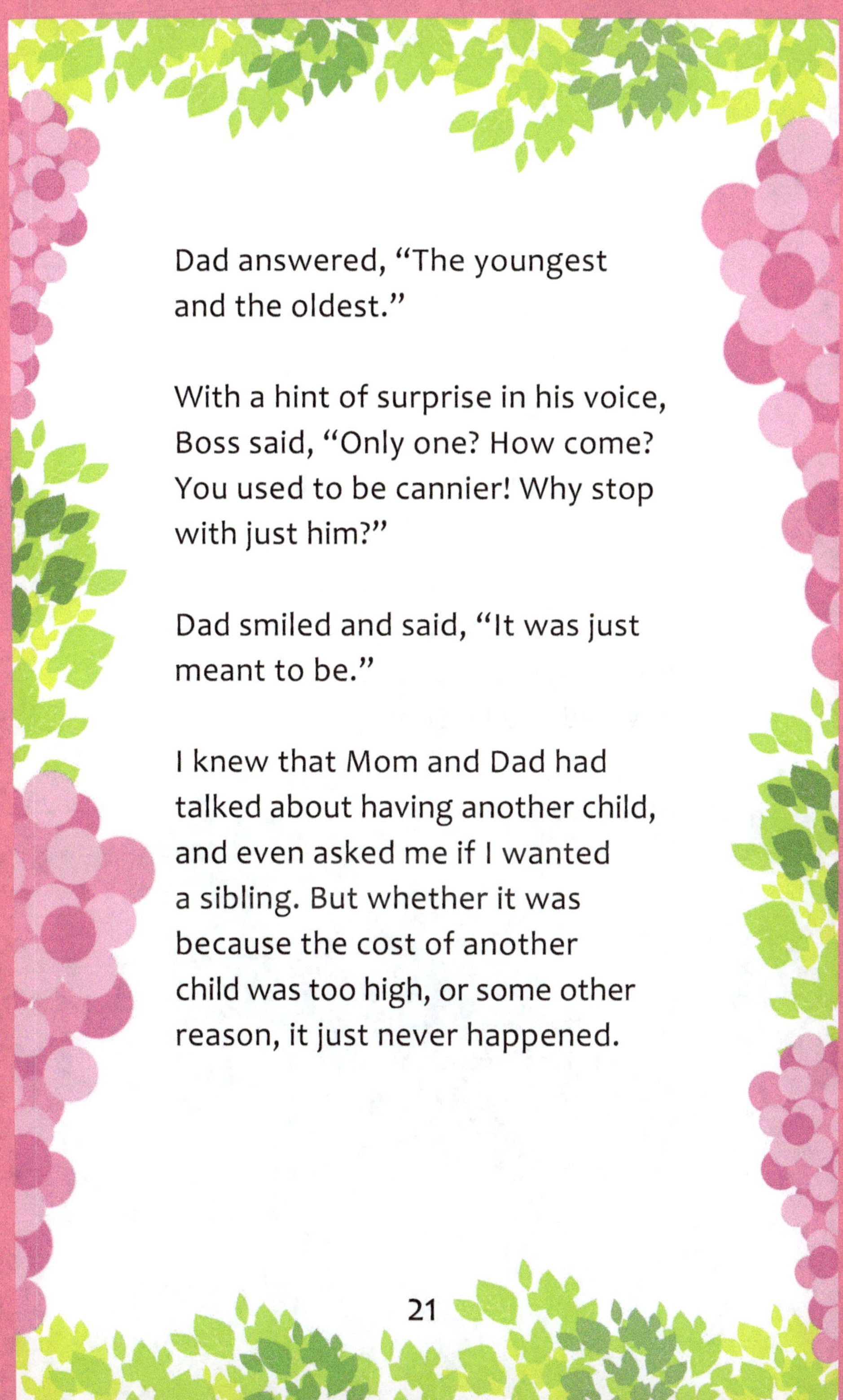

Dad answered, "The youngest and the oldest."

With a hint of surprise in his voice, Boss said, "Only one? How come? You used to be cannier! Why stop with just him?"

Dad smiled and said, "It was just meant to be."

I knew that Mom and Dad had talked about having another child, and even asked me if I wanted a sibling. But whether it was because the cost of another child was too high, or some other reason, it just never happened.

Boss patted Dad on the back and boasted that he had five sons and two daughters, each better than the other. Dad congratulated him on his prosperity and added, "You must be terribly busy!"

"Yes, indeed! But not with the kids; that's my wife's job," Boss laughed. "By the way, how did you like my humble garden?" he asked.

"I like it very much," Dad replied.
"May it always be prosperous."

"You haven't even seen all of it!
First come in for a soda then we
will take a tour around the rest of
my property before dinner,"
Boss said.

As we walked into his mansion-sized
house, Dad asked, "Where are
your wife and kids?"

"Oh, every summer I manage
the farm while they escape the
California heat and go to our
cottage," Boss said. Then he
added, "It's in Europe."

I wondered how he felt being
here all alone, just him and the
workers, and why he didn't join
his family. I was struggling with
these thoughts as I drank my
lemonade. Dad and Boss finished
their drinks in the large dining
room, then Boss went outside,
lit up a cigarette, and called
a worker to bring a car up
to the house.

Within a few minutes a shiny
grey BMW pulled up to the front
door—I immediately recognized
it as I'd seen it in a famous movie.
We all got in and set out for our
tour. Boss lit up another cigarette,
and the inside of the luxury car
soon smelled like smoke.

Boss drove us past other gardens
as beautiful as the first one.
Two large plantations were
between the gardens and a river
was flowing in between the
plantations. The area looked like
a hive of activity, a small town
with busy workers harvesting fruit.

Boss bragged non-stop about the
high quality of his products and

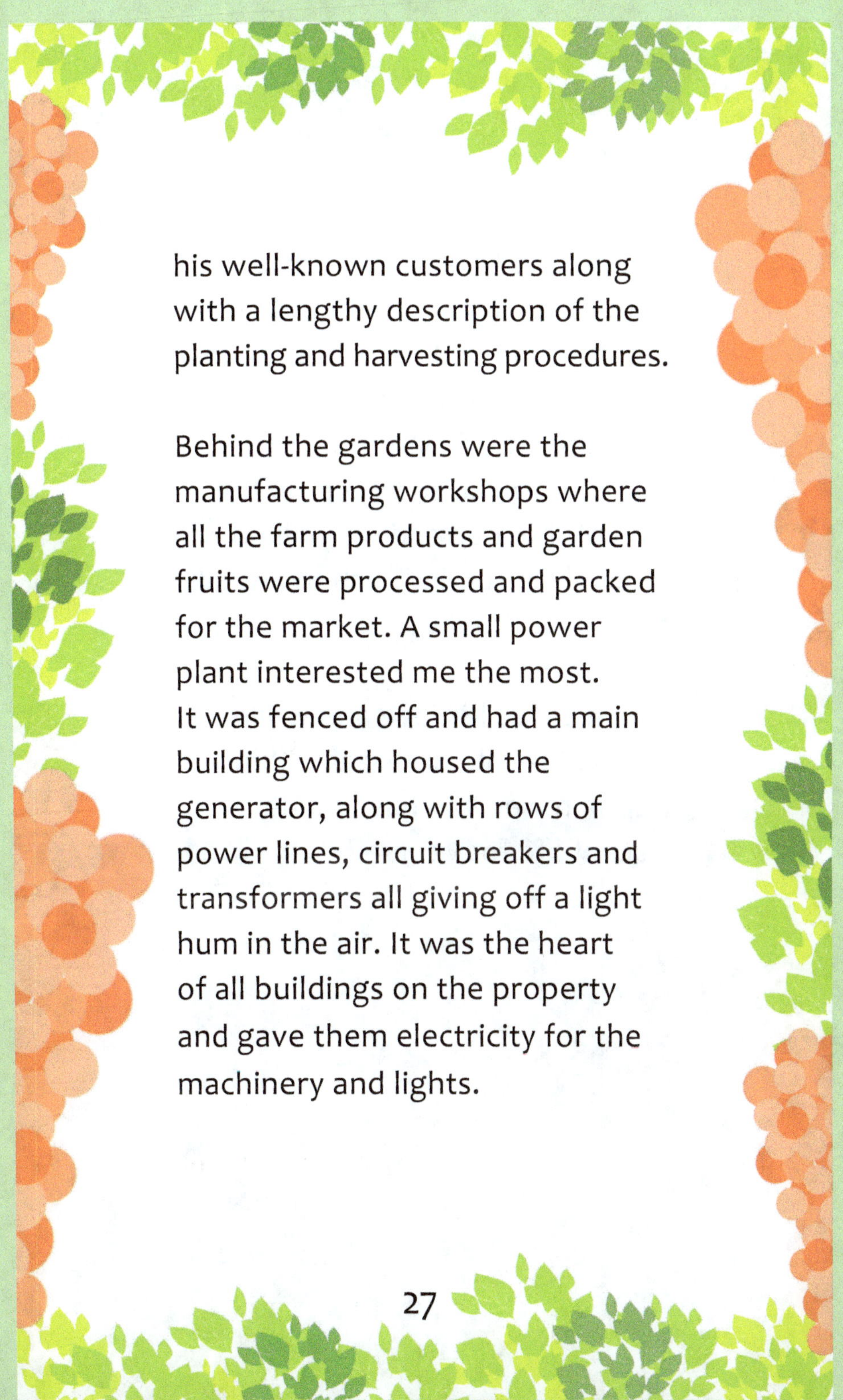

his well-known customers along with a lengthy description of the planting and harvesting procedures.

Behind the gardens were the manufacturing workshops where all the farm products and garden fruits were processed and packed for the market. A small power plant interested me the most. It was fenced off and had a main building which housed the generator, along with rows of power lines, circuit breakers and transformers all giving off a light hum in the air. It was the heart of all buildings on the property and gave them electricity for the machinery and lights.

Dad seemed like he had gotten a headache from the heat and Boss's smoking. He said he wanted to rest at the side of the nearby river to refresh himself with some cool water. Boss pulled the car to the side of the road and we walked through the underbrush to a small bank near the river.

Dad washed his face and while having his cold drink said, "I'm happy to see you have made a decent life for yourself!"

Boss put his hands on his hips and
looked out across the river at his land.

"Yes and I did it all by myself with
my own hard work. Take a look at
this place, boy," Boss said to me,
"and let it be a lesson to you: you
reap what you sow."

Boss turned back to Dad.
"Do you remember when we
were in school? You were always
the smart guy and everyone
thought I was a dope. Now look
how the world turns for me.
I'm happy with my achievements.
How about you?"

Dad said, "I am also happy with
my life, thank God."

Boss chuckled and replied,
"You don't even have a car!"

With this comment I really felt
bad, but my dad calmly replied,
"I've tried my best with what
God gave me. Sometime in future,
I may live a life much better
than now."

Boss frowned and said, "And how
is that working out for you? With
this type of job you have, you'll
never get anywhere!"

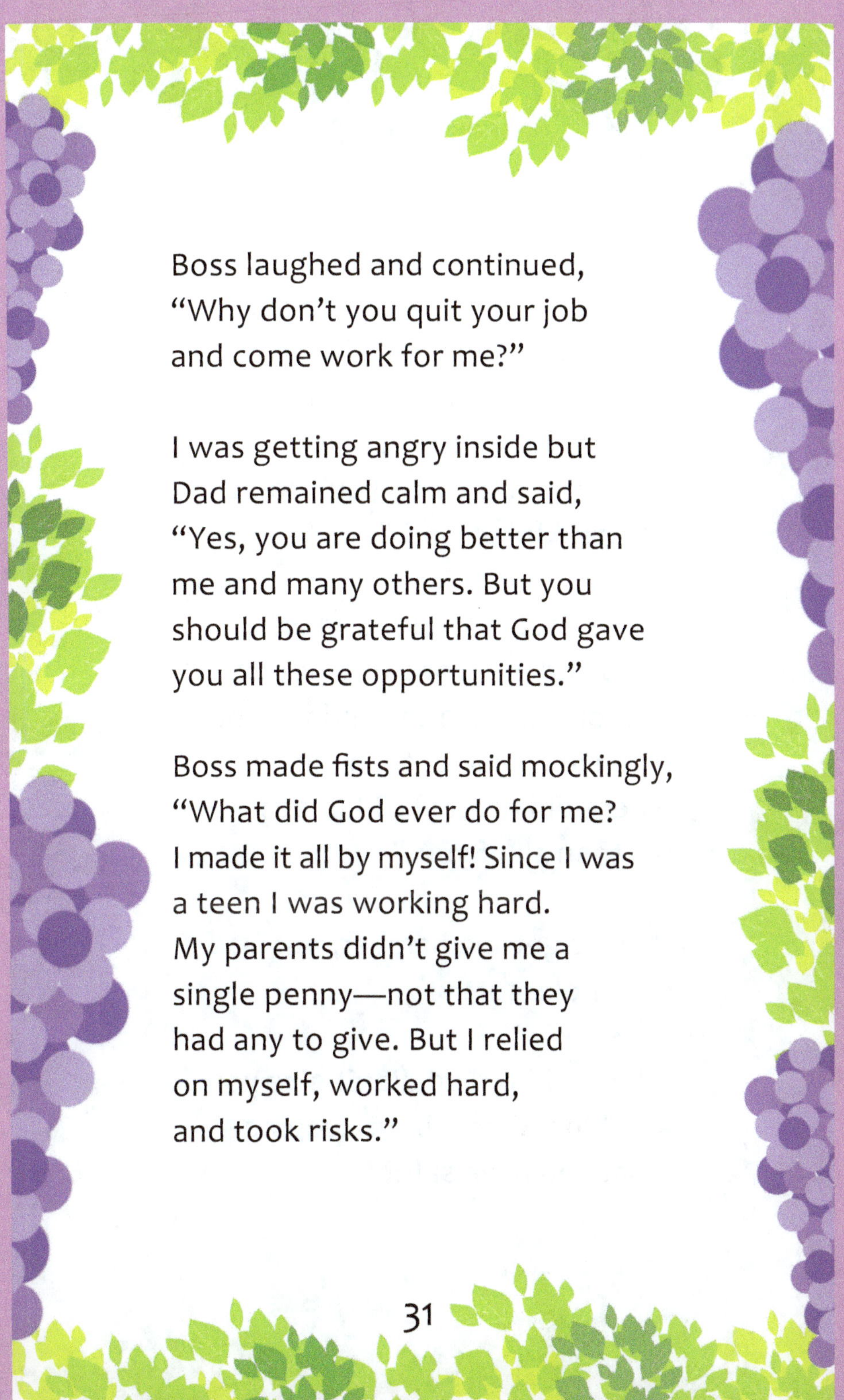

Boss laughed and continued,
"Why don't you quit your job
and come work for me?"

I was getting angry inside but
Dad remained calm and said,
"Yes, you are doing better than
me and many others. But you
should be grateful that God gave
you all these opportunities."

Boss made fists and said mockingly,
"What did God ever do for me?
I made it all by myself! Since I was
a teen I was working hard.
My parents didn't give me a
single penny—not that they
had any to give. But I relied
on myself, worked hard,
and took risks."

"Of course you worked hard,"
Dad said. "As they say: no pain,
no gain. But you were healthy
and smart enough to find your
way. You took risks and they all
paid off. That's why you should
be thankful to God."

Boss raised his voice and said,
"You and everyone else at our
school were healthy and well-off
and even smarter than me, but
where did it get you? I'm better
off than all of you."

He was getting harsher, but Dad
still spoke softly.

"If you think God didn't give you
anything, what about keeping
what you have safe?"

He asked: "Keeping it safe
from what?"

Dad relpied: "God gives and can
take away. God forbid, anything
can happen. There could be a
drought or crops could be infected
with blight or pests. But I pray
you'll be always under His protection."

I had never seen Dad speak so
frankly before.

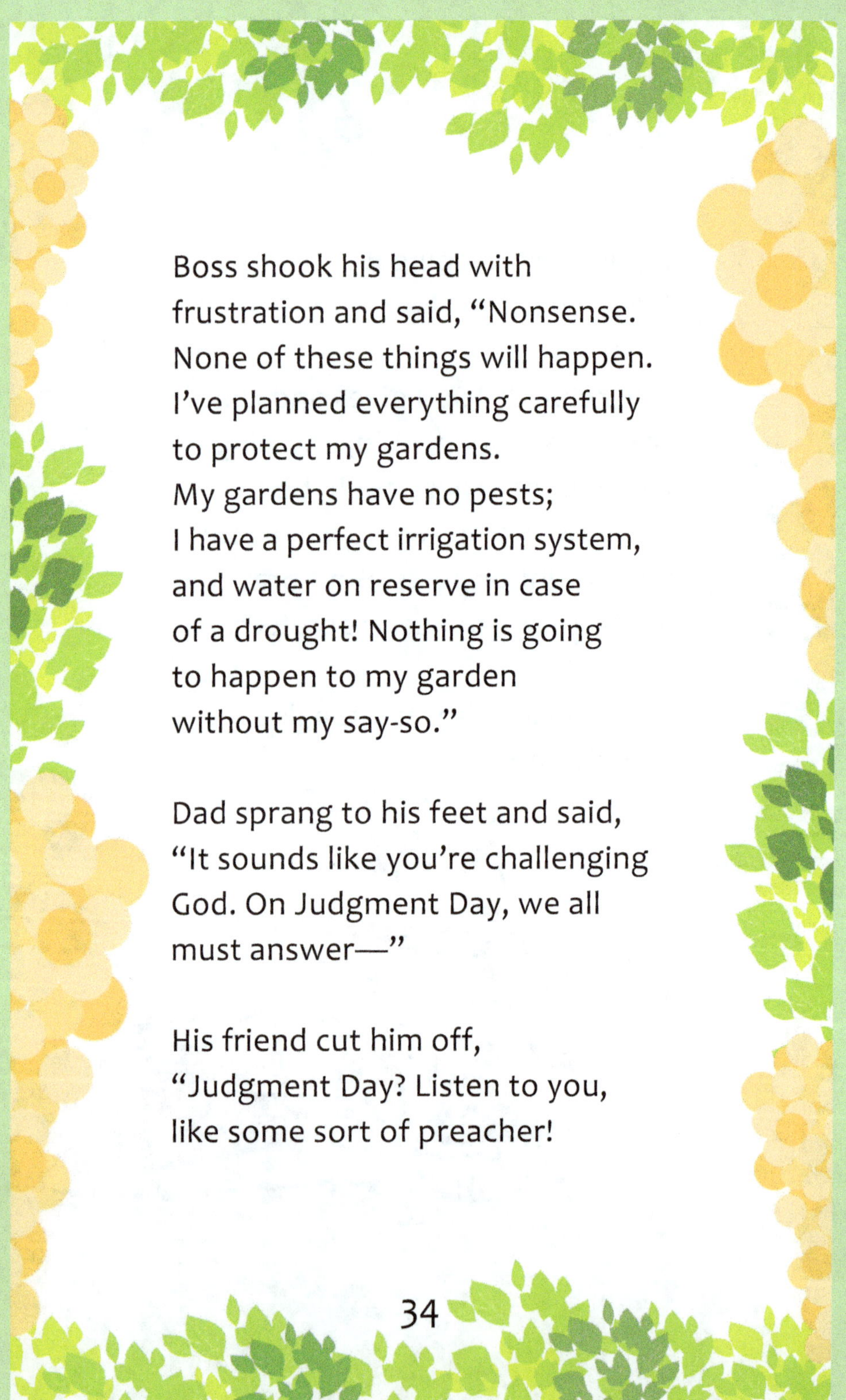

Boss shook his head with
frustration and said, "Nonsense.
None of these things will happen.
I've planned everything carefully
to protect my gardens.
My gardens have no pests;
I have a perfect irrigation system,
and water on reserve in case
of a drought! Nothing is going
to happen to my garden
without my say-so."

Dad sprang to his feet and said,
"It sounds like you're challenging
God. On Judgment Day, we all
must answer—"

His friend cut him off,
"Judgment Day? Listen to you,
like some sort of preacher!

I don't believe Judgment Day
is real; it's just something
people say to scare their kids.
Besides, if it is real, I'm certain
I'll be better off there, too."

Dad firmly stated: "If I were you,
I would be humble and grateful for
what God gave me. Don't wrong
your soul.

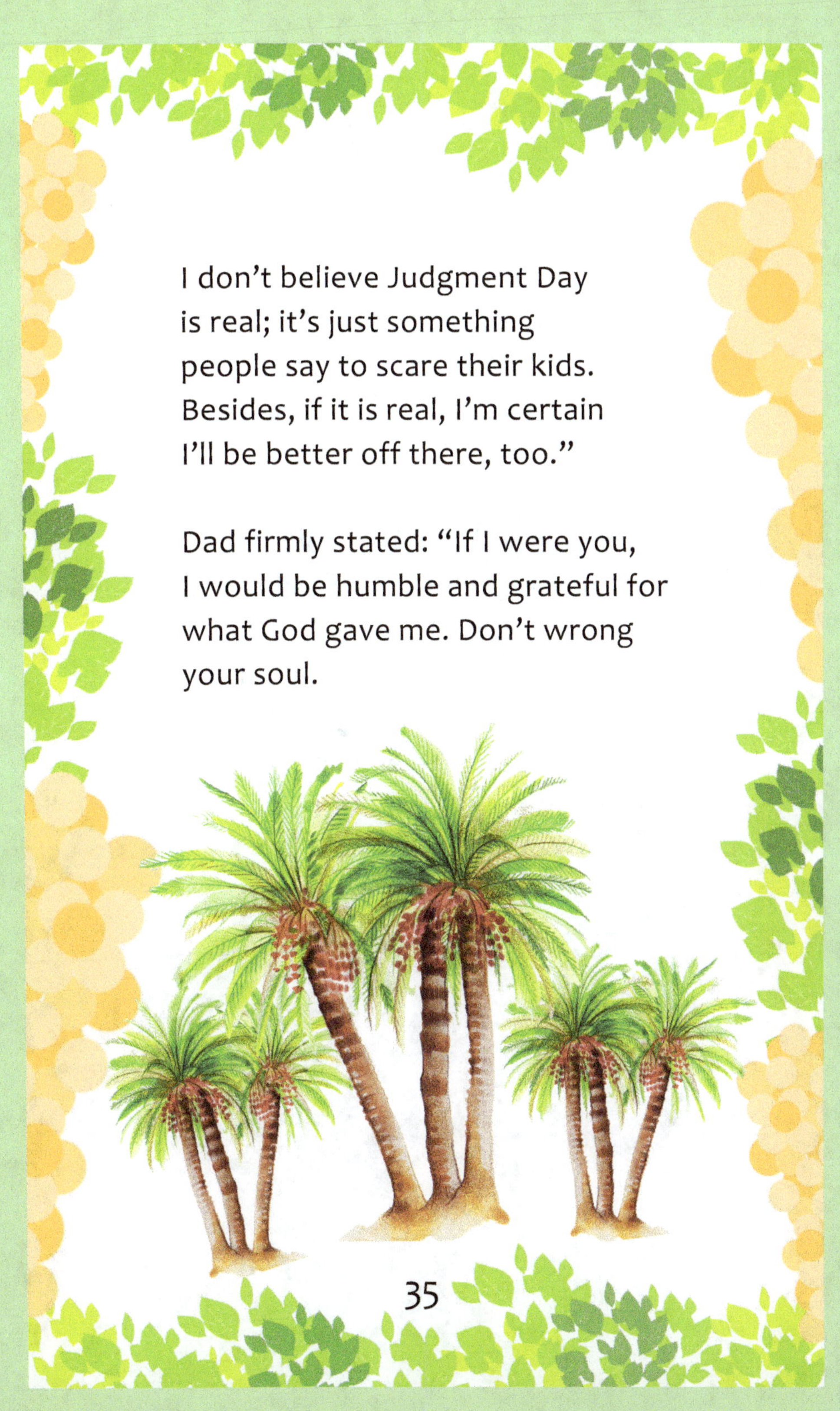

We all came from dirt and
eventually turn into dust."
Dad took a deep breath and said,
"Maybe it's better to continue
before it gets too late."

Boss simply shook his head
and all we got back to the car.
Boss continued showing off his
plantation as if nothing happened.

For the rest of the evening,
my dad didn't talk that much.

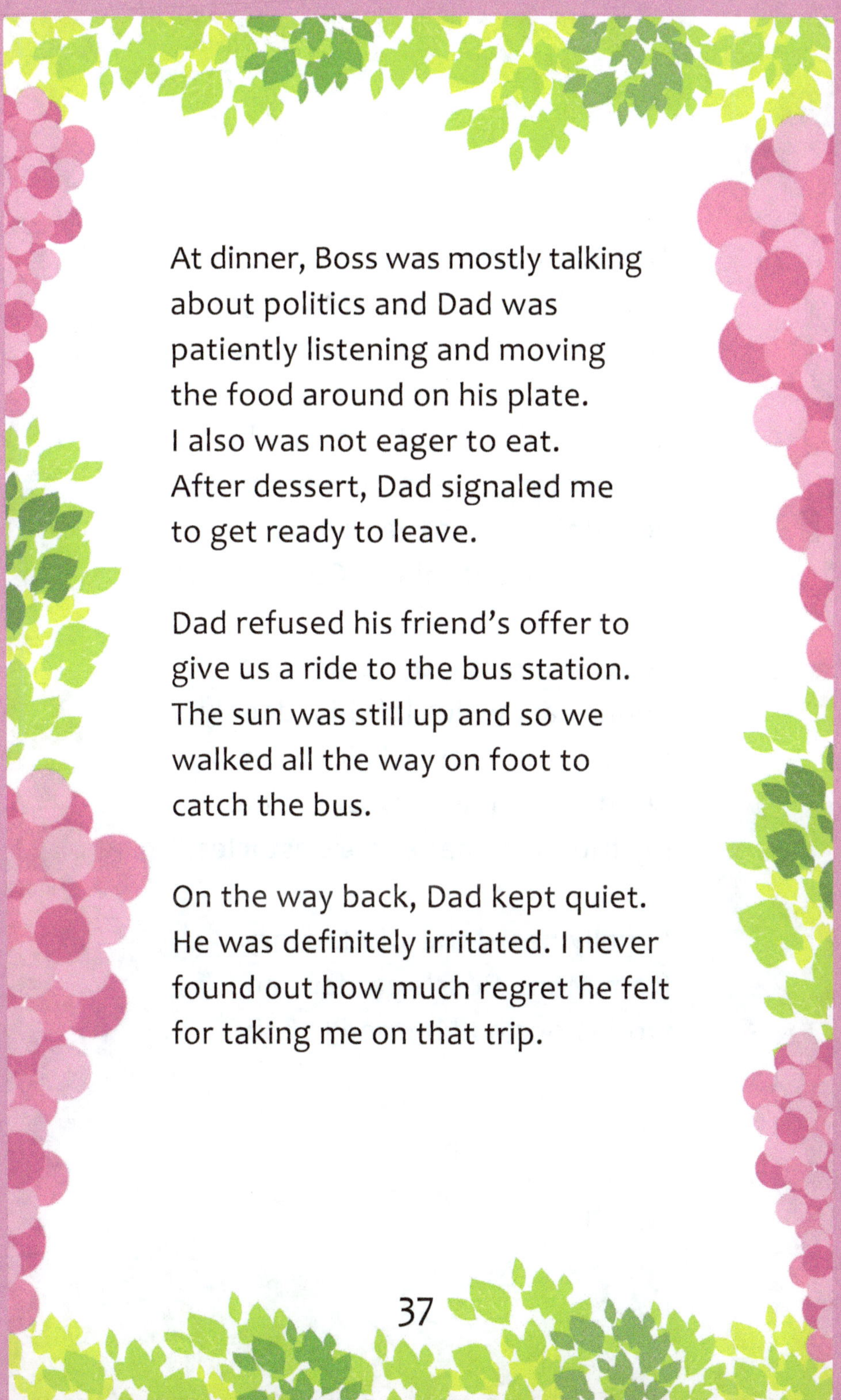

At dinner, Boss was mostly talking
about politics and Dad was
patiently listening and moving
the food around on his plate.
I also was not eager to eat.
After dessert, Dad signaled me
to get ready to leave.

Dad refused his friend's offer to
give us a ride to the bus station.
The sun was still up and so we
walked all the way on foot to
catch the bus.

On the way back, Dad kept quiet.
He was definitely irritated. I never
found out how much regret he felt
for taking me on that trip.

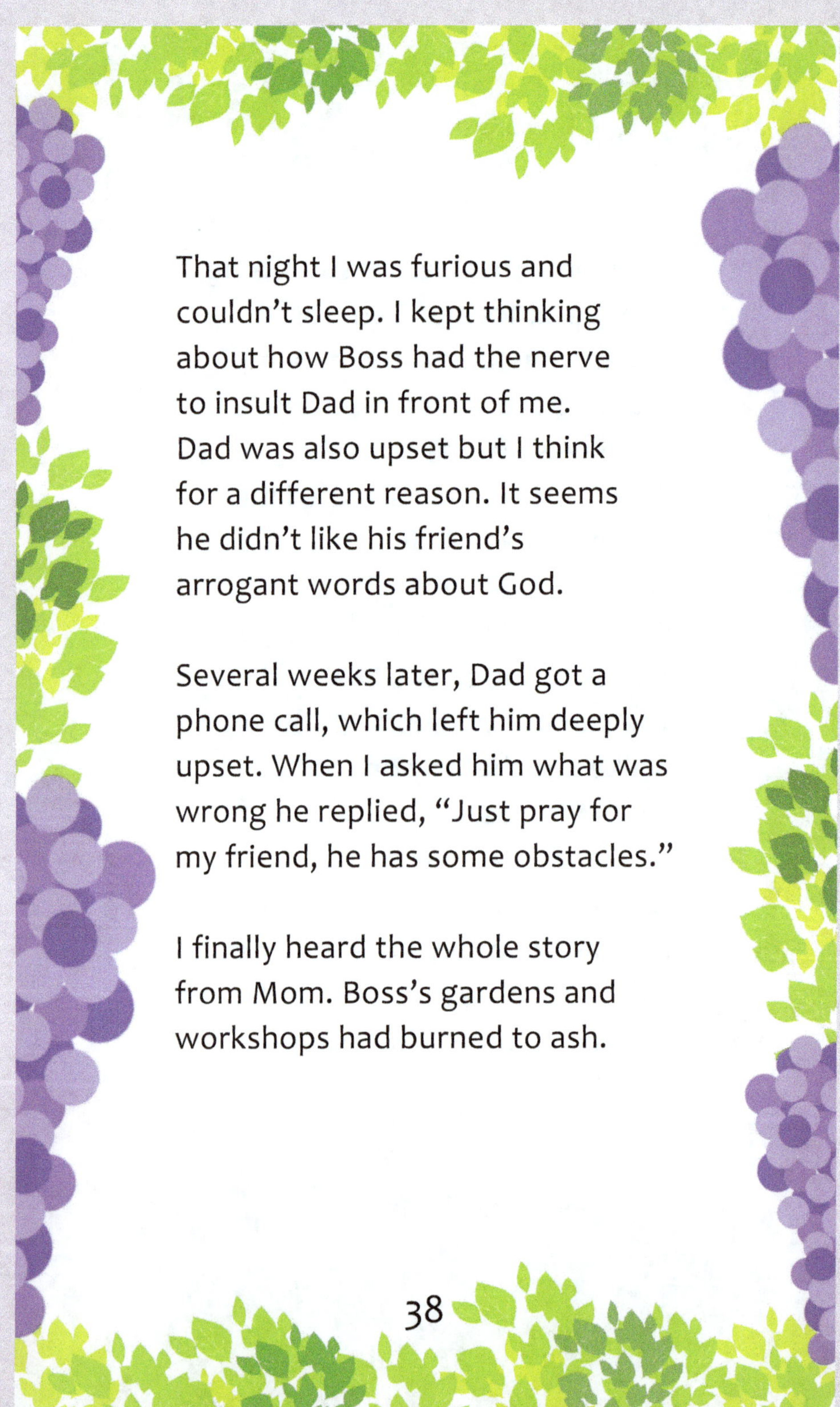

That night I was furious and couldn't sleep. I kept thinking about how Boss had the nerve to insult Dad in front of me. Dad was also upset but I think for a different reason. It seems he didn't like his friend's arrogant words about God.

Several weeks later, Dad got a phone call, which left him deeply upset. When I asked him what was wrong he replied, "Just pray for my friend, he has some obstacles."

I finally heard the whole story from Mom. Boss's gardens and workshops had burned to ash.

A spark in the power plant started a fire that quickly spread into the surrounding gardens.

Dad paid a visit to his friend to console him. I insisted on going with him. As we walked up to his property, I saw how the once-beautiful gardens had turned to a long pile of black,

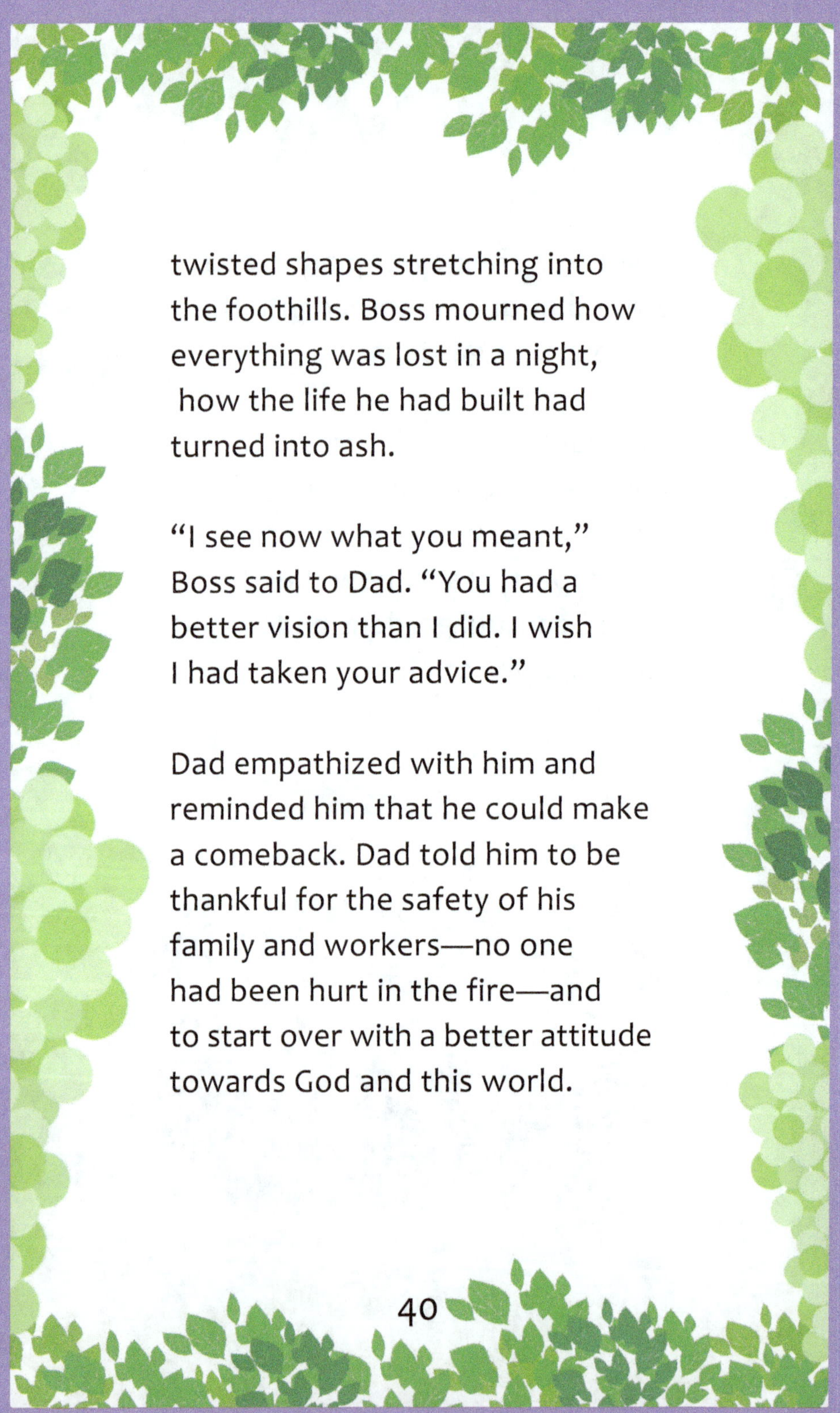

twisted shapes stretching into
the foothills. Boss mourned how
everything was lost in a night,
 how the life he had built had
turned into ash.

"I see now what you meant,"
Boss said to Dad. "You had a
better vision than I did. I wish
I had taken your advice."

Dad empathized with him and
reminded him that he could make
a comeback. Dad told him to be
thankful for the safety of his
family and workers—no one
had been hurt in the fire—and
to start over with a better attitude
towards God and this world.

We never heard from Dad's
friend after that. Since he was
traumatized, he sold his land and
move with his family to Europe.
But I would still hear Dad pray for
him throughout the years.

One day I saw a circuit board,
and all of the little components
reminded me of the power plant
on Boss's property. I became
interested in computers,
so I went to university and
studied computer engineering.
 I graduated and founded my
own company in Silicon Valley,
designing circuit boards for

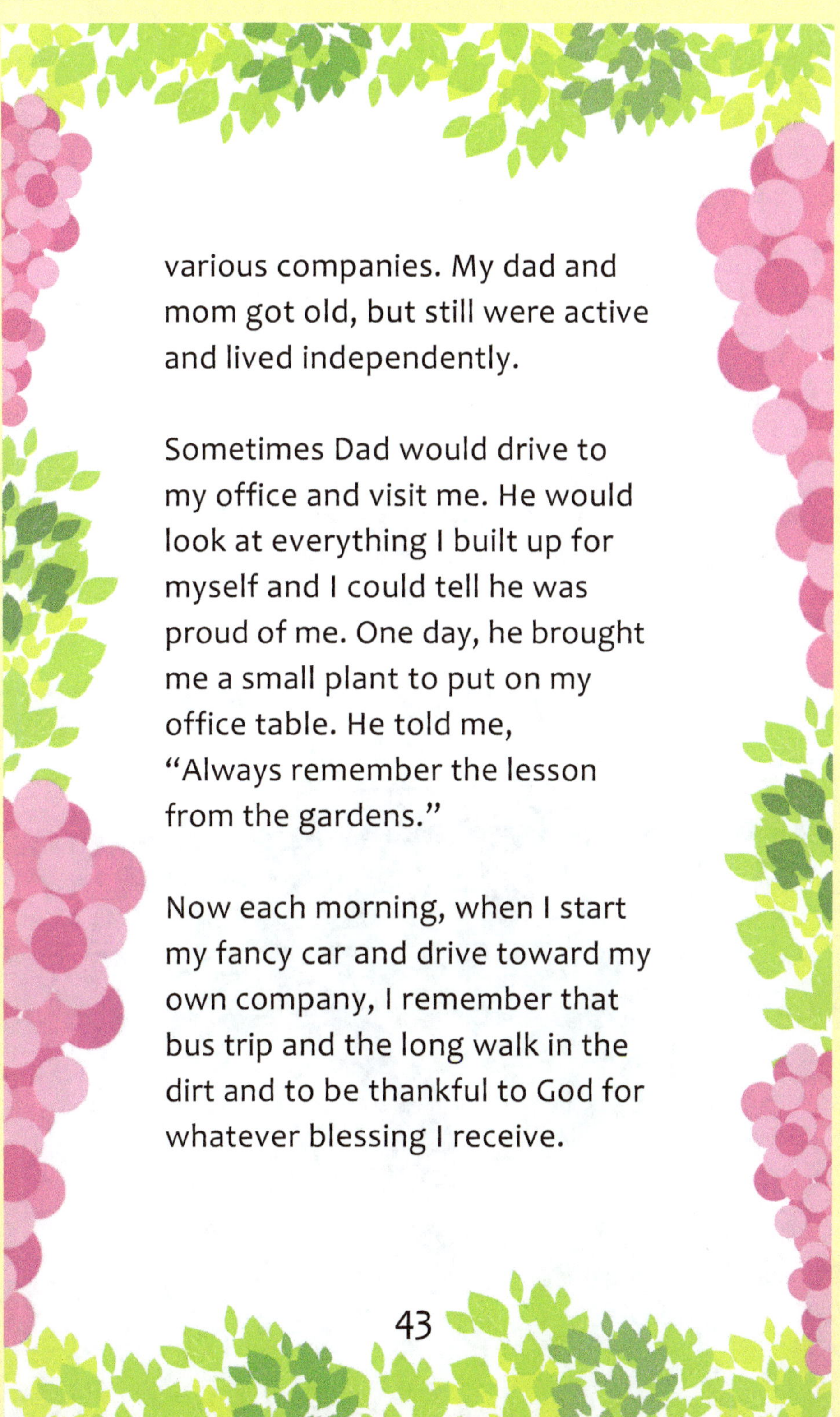

various companies. My dad and mom got old, but still were active and lived independently.

Sometimes Dad would drive to my office and visit me. He would look at everything I built up for myself and I could tell he was proud of me. One day, he brought me a small plant to put on my office table. He told me, "Always remember the lesson from the gardens."

Now each morning, when I start my fancy car and drive toward my own company, I remember that bus trip and the long walk in the dirt and to be thankful to God for whatever blessing I receive.

Comprehension Questions

Part 1:

1. Is this a non-fiction or a fiction story based
on Quranic concepts?

2. When does this story take place? Is it in
modern times or the time when the Quran
was revealed? Give your reasons.

3. Who is the narrator of the story?

4. Which people are the main characters
in the story?

5. What are some of the features of the
narrator that you can discover from
the story?

6. How would you describe Dad and his life?

7. How would you describe Boss and his life?

8. What caused all the destruction to Boss's life?

9. What did Boss believe about God and the
Day of Judgment before the accident?

10. Are such opinions that Boss had described
as *kufr* (denying the truth) or *shirk*
(associating others with God)?

11. How did the narrator's life change over
the years?

12. Dad told Boss to "start over with a better
attitude towards God and this world."
What does this mean?

13. At the end of the story, what did Dad tell
his son? And what did he mean?

Part 2:

Dear Reader,

Please study the simplified translation of Surah Al-Kahf, verses 32 to 46 in the Holy Quran, before you answer the following questions. It is important to use the printed version of the Holy Quran in its entirety.

14. Compare Surah Al-Kahf (v. 32–44) and The Gardens. Find similarities between the plot and characters of the two stories.

15. According to the story in the Quran, is the disaster that occurred to the gardens linked to the gardener's belief?

16. Can we conclude that any disaster which happens to people is the result of not being thankful to God? Is it a kind of punishment?

17. According to verse 35, how did the gardener wrong his soul?

18. Verse 39 says, in Arabic: *"Mashallah, la quwwata illa bi lah."* What does it mean?

19. Can you explain the difference in meaning between "Al-Khaliq", "Rabb", and "Allah"?

20. The Quran repeatedly mentions that Allah is also our Rabb, such as in verse 38. Why do you think this is?

21. What lessons can you learn from this story to use in your life?

22. What are you thankful for in your personal life?

Projects:

1. Please paint a picture of the gardens based on their descriptions in the Quran.

2. Please write a short drama based on the story and play it with your friends.

Reader's Guide

A Note to Dear Parents and Teachers:

Storytelling is among the most attractive means to deliver moral lessons and valuable facts to younger generations. The Holy Quran uses storytelling in some surahs to demonstrate factual evidence and teach us moral lessons. These stories are diverse and provide only the most important details to guide us.
Thus, we need to learn the Quran's unique method of expression and storytelling to comprehend its concepts or stories.

In today's entertainment-focused world, we as Muslims need to present our moral values and noble beliefs to our children more creatively and attractively. Through the years, I have learned that preaching Islam in a Western society requires different methods than the ones that may be used in Muslim countries.

To reach that goal, this book is written based on TIBS© (Teaching Islam Based on Stories), a new method of teaching in which the reader discovers and analyzes educational points while reading an entertaining story. Readers are then asked to compare and contrast the story with Quranic texts. In doing so, they gradually develop an understanding of the Quran's unique form of expression and become more familiar with this holy book. Kids will have fun discovering Quranic concepts by themselves and will pursue future learning more enthusiastically.

In the TIBS© method, religious teaching is done through indirect learning, and not by simply reporting or memorizing the canon of Islam, moralities, or history.

While using this book, it is crucial that parents/teachers refer kids to the physical written copy of the Quran in its entirety in order to get the answers for the questions accompanying each story.

It is essential to do this, rather than using
electronic or printed portions of the Quran,
so kids develop a respect for the book as a whole.

I developed the TIBS™ method in 2015, and
more comprehensive details about the TIBS™
method will be published in a separate
project, insha'Allah.

Islamic experts have reviewed this book
and I welcome your constructive suggestions
and ideas.

Please use this email address for communication:
tibs@noorhousepublication.com

Thank you

Fariba Kazemi

Learning Steps

for

"The Gardens"

Step 1:

Dear readers, first read the story then retell it with your own words.

Step 2:

Answer part 1 of the questions.

Step 3:

Read the simplified English translation of Surah Al-Kahf, verses 32 to 44.

Step 4:

Answer part 2 of the questions.

Step 5:

Painting and drama projects are started and completed.

Important

Educational

Points

1. Readers should grasp the literal meaning of the Arabic word, '*shirk*.'

Shirk is associating others with God.

It means to consider other powers as mighty as God. *Shirk* could mean worshiping idols made of stone or wood or an individual can be his/her own idol.

It could also mean while one believes in God, he/she considers other powers (including his/herself) as mighty as God.

In the Gardens story, Boss excessively believes in his merit and he was boastful about it. In a way he was worshiping himself.

2. Readers should grasp the literal meaning of the Arabic word, '*kufr*.'

Kufr is denying or hiding the truth.

Kufr exists on a spectrum. It has varying degrees. One can deny a part or the entirety of a religion.

In the Gardens story, the gardener denied the
Day of Judgment.

3. Readers should learn how believing
   or disbelieving with arrogant behavior
   influences life by producing blessing
   or disaster in their own life.
   Readers should also learn not to be
   judgmental about other people's lives.

4. Readers should learn the difference
   in meaning between "Al-Khaliq",
   "Rabb", and "Allah."

• Al-Khaliq means the Creator.
• Rabb means the One Who is the sustainer,
  the cherisher, the master, the nourisher
  and the caretaker through every stage
  of existence.
• Allah means God, the One Who is worthy
  of worship, the Ultimate reality.

Comprehension Questions and Answers

Part 1:

1. Is this a non-fiction or a fiction story based
   on Quranic concepts?

A. This story is a fiction based on the
   Quranic concepts.

2. When does this story take place? Is it in
   modern times or the time when the Quran
   was revealed? Give your reasons.

A. This story happens in modern time as it
   mentions the use of electricity, buses and
   automobiles, etc. These did not exist at
   the time of Prophet Mohammad (pbuh).

3. Who is the narrator of the story?

A. The narrator is an adult male who is
   telling a memory from his childhood.
   His name is Zach.

4. Which people are the main characters
in the story?

A. The main characters are Zach, his dad
and his dad's friend.

5. What are some of the features of
the narrator that you can discover
from the story?

A. Zach was an only child. He had a good
relationship with his parents and respected
them. He was an obedient child. Eventually,
he became a computer engineer and built
up a successful company.

6. How would you describe Dad and his life?

A. Dad was a hard-working man with a
low income who had a simple life.
He was thankful to God and was content
with what he had. He had a strong belief
in God and the Day of Judgment. He kept
his promises. He showed concern for
other people's problems.

7. How would you describe Boss and his life?

A. Boss was very wealthy. He had money
and means as well as a large family.
He made money through farming and
food manufacturing. He was rather
self-centered, boastful and arrogant.
He was a disbeliever (*mushrik / kafir*) too.

8. What caused all the destruction to Boss's life?

A. The power plant had a problem and
started a fire.

9. What did Boss believe about God and the
Day of Judgment before the accident?

A. He was boastful about his own success,
and disregarded God's will in his achievements.
On the other hand, it seems he believed in
a creator but didn't accept him as his Rabb.

Rabb means the One Who is the sustainer, the cherisher, the master, the nourisher and the caretaker through every stage of existence.

He believed that he deserved his wealth and good fortune because of his own work.

He was a denier of the Day of Judgment.

10. Are such opinions that Boss had described as *kufr* (denying the truth) or *shirk* (associating others with God)?

A. He committed both *kufr* and *shirk*. He was a *mushrik*. He may have believed in God as the Creator (see verse 36,42), but he saw himself as the main acting power in his life. It is true that he had worked hard for his fortune, but without God's will he couldn't have succeeded. Success is the result of God's will and personal efforts.

In other words he denied the role of his Rabb in his life.

He was also a *kafir*, because he denied the
Day of Judgment. When he said, "If there is
another world..." he, in fact, expressed an
improbable possibility.

11. How did the narrator's life change
over the years?

A. It is apparent that the narrator had
financial and familial success, as he
talked about his company and his life.

12. Dad told Boss to "start over with a better
attitude towards God and this world."
What does this mean?

A. People must learn that they are small
creatures with limited abilities in this
world. Their life is an opportunity for
them to better know God, to better
themselves, and avoid being arrogant
about their success.

13. At the end of the story, what did Dad tell
his son? And what did he mean?

A. He said: "Always remember the lesson
from the gardens."

This means to be thankful to God for being
successful and for all the blessings in life.

Part 2:

14. Compare Surah Al-Kahf (v. 32-44) and The
Gardens. Find similarities between the plot
and characters of the two stories.

A. In both stories, there are two friends.
One is a believer and thankful to God.
The other one is a disbeliever (*mushrik/kafir*)
who is self-centered, arrogant, and has lots
of children and assets. He showed off with
his gardens of dates and grapes, but in the
end his gardens were destroyed.

15. According to the story in the Quran, is the disaster that occurred to the gardens and the gardener's belief linked?

A. Yes. The story in Surah Al-Kahf (verses 32 to 44) shows how *kufr* and *shirk* combined with outbursts and arrogant behavior toward God could destroy one's life.

16. Can we conclude that any disaster, which happens to people, is the result of not being thankful to God? Is it a kind of punishment?

A. No, this is not correct. *Kufr* and *shirk* combined with arrogance toward God could cause disasters, but not all disasters are due to them. There are various reasons for disasters or hardships. We are not entitled to make judgments about why certain disasters happen in someone's life. For example, a plague could be a trial for believers but also a testimony of how steady they are in their beliefs.

17. According to verse 35, how did the
gardener wrong his soul?

A. He is wronging his soul since he was
boastful and arrogant towards God and
others. These negative behaviors are
crucial barriers for purification of the soul.
If a soul isn't purified, it can't grow in
virtue or gain divine rewards in the Hereafter.
He thought his wealth would last forever,
even though all things perish except for God.

18. Verse 39 says, in Arabic: "*Mashallah,
la quwwata illa bi lah.*" What does it mean?

A. "*Mashallah, la quwwata illa bi lah*" means
"As God wills, there is no power except
with God."

It is a reminder that nothing happens outside
of God's will. It is a very common phrase in
everyday Muslim speech.

19. Can you explain the difference in meaning
between "Al-Khaliq", "Rabb", and "Allah"?

A. The meanings are:
- **Al-Khaliq** means the Creator.
- **Rabb** means the One Who is the sustainer,
  the cherisher, the master, the nourisher
  and the caretaker through every stage
  of existence.
- **Allah** means the God, the One Who is
  worthy of worship, the ultimate reality.

20. The Quran repeatedly mentions that Allah
is also our Rabb, such as in verse 38.
Why do you think this is?

A. Because in pre-Islamic Arabian society,
the true meanings of these attributes
had been forgotten and replaced with
other assumptions. People knew about
Allah, the ultimate reality, but they
believed their idols would help and
sustain them in their life.

21. What lessons can you learn from this story
    to use in your life?

A. We learn that being arrogant and ignorant
    of God's blessings and not being thankful
    for them does not end well.

22. What are you thankful for in your
    personal life?

A. Readers give their own examples.

Educational **P**oints at a **G**lance

for Surah Al-Kahf
(V. 32-44)

Monotheism (Tawheed)

- Al-Khaliq (The Creator) (37)
- Rabb (Sustainer) (38)
- Allah (God) (38)
- *Shirk* (Associating others with Allah) (35,36,42)
- *Mushrik* (Those who associate others with Allah) (35,36,42)
- *Kufr* (Denying the truth) (36,37)
- *Kafir* (Denier of the truth) (36,37)

Resurrection (Ma'aad)

- Denying Judgment Day is *kufr* (36)

Ethics (Akhlaq)

- Being arrogant has bad consequences, in this world or the next (42,43)
- Not boasting about one's merit and worldly matters (wealth/children) (34)
- Not wronging yourself (35)
- Not having excessive hope in worldly things (35)
- Saying: "*Masha Allah, la quwwata illa bi lah*" (as God wills, there is no power except with God) (39)

Dear Reader,

The above pages show important teaching points of Surah Kahf (v. 32-44) at a glance when you use this book. Quranic surahs include several aspects and dimensions. These pages serve as an example and it is very probable that you discover new notions and add to the above.